MW01141391

# THE **YOUNG** ENTREPRENEURS' CLUB
# ENTERTAINMENT
## MIKE HOBBS

A+

**Smart Apple Media**

Published by Smart Apple Media,
an imprint of Black Rabbit Books
P.O. Box 3263
Mankato, Minnesota 56002
www.blackrabbitbooks.com

Published by arrangement with the
Watts Publishing Group LTD, London.

Library of Congress
Cataloging-in-Publication Data

Hobbs, Mike, 1954-
Entertainment / by Mike Hobbs.
        p. cm. -- (Young entrepreneurs club)
Includes index.
Summary: "Students interested in professional
entertainment learn what it takes to become
young entrepreneurs in the industry. Successful
entertainment moguls are spotlighted, and step-by-
step instructions are given to jump-start the thought
process of starting a business in entertainment.
Questions throughout the book challenge critical
thinking"--Provided by publisher.

ISBN 978-1-59920-921-0 (library binding)

1.  Performing arts--Juvenile literature.
I. Title.
PN1584.H63 2014
790.2--dc23

                        2012047418

Series Editor: Paul Rockett
Consultant: David Gray
Design: Simon Burrough
Picture Research: Diana Morris

Printed in the United States of America
at Corporate Graphics, North Mankato, Minnesota

P01589/2-2013

9 8 7 6 5 4 3 2 1

*Every attempt has been made to clear copyright. Should
there be any inadvertent omission please apply to the
publisher for rectification.*

Picture credits: Galyna Andrushko/Shutterstock: 27bg; Tony
Buckingham/Rex Features: 25c; Nicola Campbell/Alamy:
16; Andre Csillag/Rex Features: 23; Steve Davenport/
istockphoto: 22; Helga Esteb/Shutterstock: 35, 39c;
footagefirm.com: 27c; Patrick Frilet/hemis/Alamy: 12bl;
GaBoomswap.com: 31; www.glitch.com. © 2012 Tiny
Speck, All rights reserved: 19; Angela Hampton/Bubbles/
Alamy: 14c; Jane Hobson/Alamy: 22t; Roger Hutchings/
Alamy: 25t; Inga Ivanova/Dreamstime: 20; Marwood
Jenkins/Alamy: 28; Jonya/istockphoto: 18; KAKIMAGE/
Alamy: 22b; Justin Kasezsixz/Alamy: 14t; Keystone USA-
ZUMA/Rex Features: 26, 36; Lilu2005/Shutterstock: 5;
MakeBelieve Arts: 23t, 23b; Ken McKay/Rex Features:
32; Olga Miltsova/Shutterstock: front cover bg; Moviestore
Collection/Rex Features: 33; Sean Neal/Shutterstock: 29;
Gregory Pace/BEI/Rex Features: 11; Palsur/Shutterstock:
front cover c; Picture Perfect/Rex Features: 15b; Mark
Pink/Alamy: 12b; Pixel Youth Movement/Alamy: 7; Brian
Rasic/Rex Features: 21; Rex Features: 13,17, 39b; Screen
Gems/Everett/Rex Features: 30b; Ljupco Smokovski/
Shutterstock: 10; songkick.com: 37; John Steel/
Shutterstock: 9; Linda Steward/istockphoto: 34; Ferenc
Szelepcsenyl/Shutterstock: 24; TheDigitour.com: 15c;
Touchstone/Everett/Rex Features: 30t; World Travel/Alamy:
38; A Yakovlev/Shutterstock: 8.

# CONTENTS

# The Entertainment Industry

## That's Entertainment

What do we mean by the entertainment industry? Generally, we say that if people spend their time watching TV or a movie, or they see a band, a comedian, or a play, then they are being entertained. The same is true when people go to a club and dance to music. Even listening to music at home or playing video games is entertainment.

## Getting Involved

You can see it's a big field, with lots of money up for grabs. Everyone loves to be entertained, so there should be plenty of chances for you to get involved. Think about what forms of entertainment you enjoy—do you have a talent in this area? Would you like to be part of the entertainment industry?

**CHALLENGE**

Write out a list of what you like most about the entertainment industry. How could you make money in these areas?

# Young Entrepreneur

## Selena Gomez

There aren't many people who have had as much success at such a young age as Selena Gomez (below). Before turning 20, she had starred in many TV series, headlined in films, and formed her own band, Selena Gomez & the Scene, which has had three huge-selling albums. She is also UNICEF's youngest ever ambassador.

Selena is using her fame and **media** experience to become a young **entrepreneur** in the competitive world of filmmaking. She has formed her own production company, July Moon Productions. She has set up a deal with XYZ Films to produce and star in at least two films, while still having the freedom to work on other projects. This gives her the opportunity to explore other areas of the industry, where she might further use her skills as an entertainment entrepreneur.

**YOUR THOUGHTS**

What other parts of the entertainment industry do you think Selena might want to work in? Why?

# What Makes a Successful Entrepreneur?

## Becoming an Entrepreneur

What exactly does an entrepreneur do? He or she spends time, money, and energy developing an idea and taking a **risk** that it will make a profit. Entrepreneurs have ideas as to what people want now, and what they'll want in the future. They will try to make what people need before anyone else does.

> **CHALLENGE**
>
> You want to start a record label. Write a list of all the skills you think are necessary to succeed in this area. Think about the people you might have to work with.

## Many Routes to the Top

One of the great things about the entertainment business is that there are several ways for an entrepreneur to learn his or her skills. You can get involved with a small theater group which might lead you to a role in a big budget movie. Maybe you'll start managing a folk singer who plays at local bars and clubs, and later use these experiences to manage a stadium rock act in the future. And because of the explosion of new media (especially social media), there are lots of different untrod paths to success in the industry.

There are many qualities you need to be successful. Perhaps the most important of these is a real passion for what you're doing and a strong determination to succeed. If you can match these with the ability to work hard, then you have the makings of an entrepreneur.

Which part of the industry attracts you?

# Young Entrepreneur
## Sean Parker

Sean Parker's hobby as a child was computer programming and computer hacking. He began computer programming at the age of 7, and was arrested for hacking by the age of 16. A few years later, along with Shawn Fanning, he **launched** Napster, and the music industry was changed forever. Napster allowed people to share music files online for free. The major record labels didn't like this. Napster was breaking **copyright** laws, and eventually it was shut down. However, Napster was the fastest growing business of all time— within one year it had tens of millions of users.

Since Napster, Sean has become a serial entrepreneur, investing his money and experience in a large number of start-up companies he believes in. Plaxo, Friendster, Facebook, Founders Fund, Airtime—these are just a few of the businesses in which he has played a leading role. And what about his relationship with the music industry? Well, he is now a major **investor** in Spotify, a legal music-sharing platform similar to Napster. This time he works together with record labels, so that people can listen to unlimited music and not break the law.

**YOUR THOUGHTS**

What would be the advantage of investing in many businesses rather than just one?

# Deciding on an Idea

## Do What You Love

OK, here's the fun part. You've got to decide what you'd like to do. Could it be working in film, TV, or the arts? Maybe you'd like to be more in the spotlight as a ventriloquist or a singer. Perhaps you've already started on a career as a DJ.

There are plenty of opportunities for you to be the person who helps others entertain people. Do you want to start a comedy club, a dance club, or manage a band? You could provide the organization and the support to make money out of others' work.

Think about what entertains you and what you and others are willing to pay for.

You need to examine all your ideas closely until you hit on the right one. Talk to your friends, your family, or anyone whose opinion you value and see what they have to say. You don't have to act on their advice, but it might give you some ideas before you start getting serious.

**CHALLENGE**

What do you feel is likely to be the next big thing in entertainment over the next three years? Write down three ways you could make money from it.

# Young Entrepreneur
## SB.TV

British online channel SB.TV began with a Christmas present: Jamal Edwards (left) was given a video camera. In 2007, he began filming random stuff and uploading it to YouTube. The fact that he got 1,000 views for some footage of foxes in his London backyard showed him that the Internet was worth using for other interests—such as grime music. Jamal's research showed that grime, a blend of British garage and hip-hop, was only being covered on YouTube and independently produced DVDs. He saw a gap in the market to share the music he loved.

Jamal filmed rappers whenever and wherever he could and uploaded them onto his channel, SB.TV. The channel soon had lots of followers, but Jamal believed he could be even more successful. So he also took footage of stars who were already successful, such as Justin Bieber, Nicki Minaj, and Ellie Goulding. Although this lost him some hardcore supporters, the gamble paid off. SB.TV now has over 50,000 users, makes money from advertising sold on the channel, and has a deal signed with Sony RCA.

**YOUR THOUGHTS**

Where did Jamal's ideas come from? Do you think he was right to upload music that was not grime music?

# Checking Out Your Market

## Finding Out about the Business

You've probably heard the saying that "there's no business like show business." Well, it may be exciting, but it's also very hard. People can be slow to spend money when it comes to entertainment. You should research your **potential market** thoroughly to make sure that you can make money from it. **Market research** is divided into two different types:

**Primary research:** new information you gather from direct observation or questions to the public.
**Secondary research:** existing information you can get from sources such as the Internet or the library.

## Asking Questions

There are plenty of ways you can get **feedback** about whether you're onto a winner. It's a good idea to check out places that attract the audience that you want.

Let's say that you're thinking of putting together your own online database of short films made by friends at your college. You could ask people outside a movie theater whether they'd be interested in seeing them, and ask other questions that may prove useful. You could also do some secondary research on the Internet to see if there is anything similar available.

**CHALLENGE**

You're setting up an online movie database. You want to find out what types of movies people will pay to watch on it. Write three questions to ask your potential audience.

# Young Entrepreneur
## The DigiTour

Meridith Valiando (below, center) is a young record company entrepreneur who saw the way in which the music audience was moving—and acted on it. She was working at a major record label and felt that the old ways of finding and promoting artists were out of touch with their audience. She saw the popularity of YouTube and became convinced that artists and groups who attracted interest online could sell more concert tickets. So she set up a business to turn site hits into hit tours.

The record industry doubted Meridith could make it work, but regardless, she co-founded the DigiTour. DigiTour is a five-week concert tour featuring unsigned acts that have been successful on YouTube (and have at least 2 billion views). Finding sponsorship from beverage company

Neuro, she has proved the doubters wrong and people have flocked to the shows. Meridith's success is a great example of someone with inside knowledge spotting the impact that new media can have on a stagnating business.

**YOUR THOUGHTS**

What was it about YouTube that Meridith saw as being important for the music industry?

# Attracting Funds
## to Start Up

## Finding Funding

Whatever you decide to do, you will need money to get started. There may be grants for young entrepreneurs in your area. Check online or at libraries to see if you qualify for any. Otherwise, money can come from many sources, such as parents, banks, or other lenders. In nearly all cases, they will want you to agree to give them something in return for funding you.

## Creating a Financial Plan

You will stand a better chance of getting investors if you've got a proper **financial plan** showing what these **backers** will get in return—and when they'll get it. The details of what you'll need to put in this plan are:

- The amount you need to invest in equipment. For example, if you plan to make a short film, how much money do you need for the camera and to rent an editing suite?

- The amount you'll have to pay on weekly running **costs**. This may include salaries, electricity, or materials.

- The other estimated special costs, such as marketing.

- The predicted sales for your first year.

Also include the likely date of first payment to investors. You may have to revise this plan, but it's good to be clear about what's involved.

**CHALLENGE**

You are putting on a play and plan to make money on ticket sales. However, you need some cash up-front for costumes. Write a list of all the sources you might approach to get the investment money. Put them in order, starting with those you would get the most money from to those you would get the least.

# Young Entrepreneurs
## RKA Records

Ryan Ashmore and Liam Webb set up RKA Records in November 2010 after Ryan had seen musician MarQ Figuli while on vacation. Ryan convinced Liam to set up a record label together and sign MarQ. The new label bosses were just 18 years old.

However, recording can be a slow and costly process, and both Ryan and Liam needed money to keep going. So they went on the BBC TV program *Dragons' Den* to see if they could raise some money. They accepted a deal of $80,000 in exchange for a 79% share of RKA, even though it was a much tougher deal than they hoped for. The TV appearance helped them meet many musicians, including the band Reconnected, who signed with them, and Janet Devlin (right) who appeared on Britain's *X Factor*. The label has since been renamed Bannatyne Music, and they continue to search for the next big artist to sign.

**YOUR THOUGHTS**

Do you think Ryan and Liam were wise to accept the deal with *Dragons' Den*? What would you have done and why?

# Does It Work in Practice?

## Product Testing

You have now decided on an idea and you have done some research to show that it is what people want. You've also got the financial backing to start on your plans. But does your idea actually work when you put it to the test? This is another important side of market research, known as **product testing**.

If it's an online application (app), are there any glitches? Try it out on some members of the public. You could set up a formal **user group** (which may involve some expense), or if you're lucky, get some friends to try every aspect of the app for free. You will need to find out whether any problems might come up.

## Practice Makes Perfect

It may seem as though there's a lot of time spent in research, but it's a great showbiz tradition. Think of rehearsals for plays, TV, films, and concert tours.

Everybody in the entertainment industry puts in the time perfecting their craft, and you shouldn't be any different.

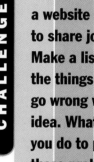

**CHALLENGE**

You are launching a website set up to share jokes. Make a list of all the things that may go wrong with your idea. What could you do to prevent these problems from happening?

## Young Entrepreneur
### Glitch

In September 2011, *Glitch*, the popular game of a "world within a world" was launched. It quickly built a fanbase and word spread fast. But founder Stewart Butterfield believed that his team of developers could make *Glitch* easier for new members to play and that they could provide players with even more activities.

In short, *Glitch* had glitches. Butterfield's solution was to "unlaunch" the game, or stop it from being used while they worked on the changes.

What were the benefits of doing this? *Glitch* offered players their money back, showing they are an honest and professional company. At the same time, it showed that *Glitch* is a company that keeps high standards.

Sadly, Glitch came to an end in 2012. Butterfield again offered refunds, and the positive publicity he's earned will only benefit his next venture.

**YOUR THOUGHTS**

How might "unlaunching" *Glitch* be a bad move in the long term?

# Back to the Drawing Board

## Changes and Improvements

All right, you've done your product testing and learned quite a lot. You should have a pretty good idea of what will work and what won't. The important thing to do now is to polish what you have until it really shines.

## Starting Small

Even once rehearsals are over, you may still need to improve. Many shows start in small theaters, and music tours begin with small gigs before opening in larger venues. This gives the opportunity to test what the audience thinks and then smooth out any mistakes. This might require rewriting the script or even recasting the actors.

If you are launching a digital product, you may want to provide access to a **closed community** (a limited number of users) before going big.

▲ It's worth taking your time to consider every small detail. Is the color on your logo exactly the right color?

Facebook started out by giving access to colleges and universities before going global. By reaching a smaller audience first, you have the perfect chance to develop further before hitting the bigger market and the bigger money.

**CHALLENGE**

Sometimes products get released to the public, and only later are problems discovered. In some cases, these products have to be recalled. Imagine you have put on a comedy show. No one laughed, and the audience complained. What would you do?

# Young Entrepreneur

## Lana Del Rey

It was clear from her early days that New Yorker Lizzy Grant was a talented singer-songwriter. With her fashion model good looks, it seemed she was going to be a star. She released her first EP, *Kill Kill*, in 2008, and her first LP, *Lana Del Ray a.k.a Lizzy Grant*, in 2010. But almost as soon as it had been released, she withdrew the record from the market. Why?

This is a classic example of a young entrepreneur removing a product, polishing it, and relaunching—it just so happened the product was herself. Basically, Lizzy had decided she could improve her songs, her voice, and her image, and have an even greater chance at success. With a slight alteration to the spelling, she returned as Lana Del Rey in the summer of 2011, and her single "Video Games," became an enormous hit on YouTube. Her follow-up songs, "Blue Jeans" and "Born to Die," have also attracted huge attention, and her LP (also called *Born to Die*) came out in January 2012. The change worked, and Lizzy's Lana Del Rey has become a successful **brand**.

**YOUR THOUGHTS**

Do you think Lizzy should have continued with her first attempt at success rather than withdrawing from it? Why?

# Size Up Your Rivals

## You've Got Competition

You'll be really eager to get going by now, but there's still one last vital piece of research you will have to do. Unless your idea is so new that there is nobody else out there like you, you're going to have **rivals** who'll be chasing the same customers. You need to find out what you are up against!

Who are you going to compete with? If you're opening a club, look around. What other clubs are in the area? If you're developing a movie or play, what other films and shows are people going to see? If you're presenting a music project, which bands or singers are doing well? What other video games are people playing if you're in that field?

▲ **If you're a comedian, how can you get more laughs than the comedian that the audience watched before you?**

## Compete to Win

Look carefully at what your direct **competitors** are doing. Note what's good about them, what's not so good, and learn from both. How can you improve what they're doing? Competition can be great at making you work harder, with rivals setting a standard for you to beat.

**CHALLENGE**

You want to start a film review website with a booking service. Research the Internet to find out who your rivals will be. What are they doing well?

# Young Entrepreneur
## Music Arsenal

Music Arsenal is a web site that helps manage musicians and bands who are not part of a big music label. It offers assistance with planning and promoting. Jimmy Winter from Omaha, Nebraska, got the idea from his experience as a booking agent for bands. He knew that if musicians wanted to compete against the bigger rival groups, they would need the same help, support and information.

The service gives band members and managers a clear view of all their contacts, tasks, schedules, expenses, and goals. They have constant access to this information. Jimmy knew that he was setting up a business to compete with big music labels, but by working with the **indie** market, an area the bigger labels might ignore, he has been successful, and the business continues to grow.

**YOUR THOUGHTS**

If Music Arsenal were a rival company to you, how could you make your company more noticeable?

# Budgeting for Success

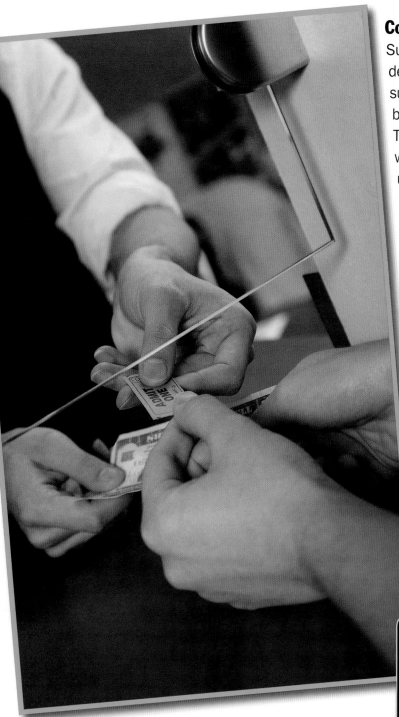

### Counting Costs

Success in the entertainment industry depends on very tight **budgeting**. Make sure you're adding up all the costs of your business, however small they may seem. Think about what your expenses are and who you have to pay. You don't want any unexpected headaches!

### Profit and Cash Flow

Two important things to think about in your venture are **profit** and **cash flow**. The greatest idea counts for nothing if you can't keep it going. You must make a profit if you want to stay in business.

You also need to see that money is coming in regularly, as well as and going out to cover your running costs. In difficult economic times, the largest cause of company failure is not an empty order book, but late payments and unpaid bills.

**CHALLENGE**

You're setting up your own theater company to tour colleges and schools. List all the ways in which you could make sure cash comes in regularly to the business.

# Young Entrepreneur
## MakeBelieve Arts

Trisha Lee (left) founded London-based MakeBelieve Arts in 2002. Her aim was to provide lively theater and education programs to schools to help children develop their creative skills.

The company has been successful in achieving its goals, but naturally, finding the money to pay for these programs has been difficult.

The solution Trisha has come up with is to find individual backers for separate projects. So, for instance, the Wellcome Trust, the Austin & Hope Pilkington Trust, the Ironmongers' Company, and the Mercers' Company each supported separate programs in 2012. In the past, Trisha has gained funding from arts councils, banks, and private foundations. She finds money in all kinds of places and is always looking for more backers to support her projects.

**YOUR THOUGHTS**

What costs would Trisha Lee include in a budget for her business?

# Putting a Team Together

## Teamwork

In the entertainment industry, teamwork is vital. So many projects involve a variety of people with different skills working together. Film crews, theater companies, choirs, orchestras, and opera companies are all obvious examples of teamwork in action. In each of these groups, there are many different skills and talents needed for success. It's important to get good people working for you, and you need to be sure that they have the right skills to make it work.

▲ **In an orchestra, everyone has to work well together for the music to sound right.**

**CHALLENGE**

**You want to start a comedy club in your neighborhood. What sort of people would you get to help you, and why? What skills would you be after?**

Ideally, you'll want everyone to work well together in the team, so you'll want to hire the type of person who will fit in. Are they cheerful? Do they get along with other people? Is it important for them to have a good sense of humor? Of course, they may be the nicest and most popular person in the room, but don't forget they also need to be able to do the job.

# Inspiring Entrepreneur
## Cameron Mackintosh

London's Cameron Mackintosh (bottom right) is the most successful producer of theater musicals today. But he learned about the importance of teamwork in putting together musical productions by working first as a stage hand, and then as an assistant stage manager on the national tour of *Oliver!* He understood from the start how important everyone was to the creation of a musical, and he's well known for working closely with his creative teams. When he was in his early 20s, he took the steps to become a producer of musical shows.

Cameron went on to produce many musicals including *Cats*, *Phantom of the Opera*, and *Les Misérables*, which have all been hits on Broadway and in London's West End, as well as across the world. These productions all follow the same staging, design, and musical arrangements wherever they are put on, so they are always of a high standard. To carry out what is required, it is essential to have an effective team. By emphasizing the importance of teamwork, Cameron continues to apply the lessons he learned early in his career.

**YOUR THOUGHTS**

What are the benefits of Cameron Mackintosh working his way up in business by filling different roles?

# Learn to Be Decisive

## Making Decisions

You're running a large **multimedia** entertainment project and all the creative people are telling you their point of view. It's important to listen to advice from others who may have more experience than you, but never forget that you're making the decisions. People in the entertainment business have strong opinions and aren't afraid to express them, but you are in charge. Consider your options carefully. You may be a magician, but you can't make miracles happen—make sure your decisions are practical.

Your research in the market should help you make the right decisions. A few mistakes are forgivable in the early days, but you will need to learn from these fast. You need to show confidence in what you decide to do. This will also encourage those around you to do as you ask.

**CHALLENGE**

**Every day we make lots of decisions without even realizing it. We decide on the route we walk and the food we eat. Make a list of all the decisions you made today, then think about the decisions you didn't make or wish you'd made.**

# Young Entrepreneur
## Footage Firm

Joel Holland (below) of Virginia founded his company, Footage Firm, in 2001 when he was 16. He started by selling film footage on eBay that he had shot of sunsets while he was on vacation in Hawaii. Soon he realized that there was a big worldwide market for similar stock film—said to be worth about $1 billion each year. So Joel brought together a team of 25 videographers and began to record as much film footage as possible.

Joel has found a way to make sure his company grows and stays on top. What he does is offer some royalty-free stock film footage free of charge (except postage) to companies. His decision to give away footage for free was seen as a risk and is a decision many companies don't make. However, it gets customers to use his company, and the name of Footage Firm becomes known. Footage Firm can then make money by selling material from their wider collection of film footage, as well as from the supply of sound effects they sell. Joel was named one of *Business Week's* top 25 Entrepreneurs of 2006 and received the Small Business Entrepreneur of the Year title for 2007.

**YOUR THOUGHTS**

Why was giving away free footage a good decision for Joel to make?

# Creating a Marketing Plan

## In the Mix

As you get closer to your launch, you have to make sure that you are doing all you can to sell as many tickets or downloads as possible. Figure out a **marketing plan**, adding in all the different parts of the marketing mix—and make sure your plan is linked to the budget you prepared earlier.

**CHALLENGE**

You are opening a new music and arts club venue. Think of as many creative ways you could promote it.

Once you've decided on your plan, you need to put it into action. To do this, it's often helpful to think of the four Ps:

**Product:** What your product offers and what makes it different from its competition. How is your platform game different from the bestsellers on the market?

**Price:** What your customers will be prepared to pay. Will you offer discounts to students or offer a limited free trial period?

**Place:** How and where you are going to sell your product. Is your music only going to be available online or in formats such as vinyl or CD?

**Promotion:** How to reach your market most effectively. This can include advertising, **public relations** (PR), sales promotions, and by creating a brand. How can you best get your comic book series talked about?

## Young Entrepreneurs
### Musicane

Vikramaditya Jain, Sudhin Shahani, Kale McNaney, and Josh Zibit are four Internet entrepreneurs from Venice, California who founded Musicane in 2006. It is a music and social shopping and discovery network, offering services that allow users to buy, sell, or share music online. This is a very tough market, and the co-founders have used two well-proven strategies as part of their marketing plan.

The first is technical know-how: every user gets their own Musicane widget, which can be embedded in blogs, web sites, and social network pages. The users reach their online communities and share commission on music sold. The second is to provide great content and to use various music stars to back their service. For instance, Will.i.am from the Black Eyed Peas (above) was made Musicane's head of marketing in 2006, and the well-publicized Musicane partnership with Lil Wayne spread 54,000 widgets in a week. The company is also an MP3 retail partner with the Universal Music Group and the Orchard, as well as with over 50,000 independent artists.

**YOUR THOUGHTS**

What difference do you think it made having celebrities with Musicane?

# Getting Known

## Attention!

Does your audience know about your plans? It doesn't matter how good the show is if no one's there. And if you're launching an online site, are your target customers aware of what you're doing? Two of the main ways to spread news are advertising and PR. Think about what works for your product. If you are opening a club, you might use a local newspaper to attract people living close by. If you are managing comedy acts, perhaps their jokes only need to be heard, and so they can be broadcast on the radio.

Plan your **advertising campaign** with great care, and support it with some public relations and other promotional work. You can run competitions in the local paper for free tickets or offer reduced price previews. You may also want to offer free trials, sales promotions, or samples as ways of showing your product in the best light.

**CHALLENGE**

You've decided to launch a DVD trading site so people can swap their old movies. How do you go about getting publicity for it?

# Young Entrepreneur
## GaBoom

Jessica Ratcliffe (left) from Guildford, England used some traditional methods to make sure her former business was a publicity hit. GaBoom was an online user-to-user game trading service that Jess set up because, like many others, she was finding new (or even secondhand) video games expensive. It was a simple user matching service where people listed the games they had and ones they wanted, and they were put in touch with gamers who they could swap with.

When it came to publicizing her site, Jess used two promotional tools. First, she won the UK National Varsity Pitching Competition for 2010, which gave her company and her confidence a boost (and put $60,000 in her bank account!). Next, she applied for a spot on the BBC *Dragons' Den* TV show and experienced tough questioning from other entrepreneurs. She didn't gain investment from them, but she did pick up useful experience and publicity.

**YOUR THOUGHTS**

List the advantages and disadvantages of Jessica appearing on *Dragons' Den* to promote her site.

# Launch Time!

## Opening Night

All the build-up is coming to an end at last. It's time to focus all your attention on your opening night or big launch. One obvious way to get interest from the media is to throw a party. Everyone in the entertainment world loves a good party, but don't let your message get lost in all the fun. You don't want all your hard work and planning to go to waste.

Your opening night is one of the best chances you have of communicating with your **target audience**. It's the most obvious example of your marketing strategy in action. Make as big a noise as you can, and make sure you keep up your energy and momentum. You'll want reviews and feedback from blogs, Facebook, Twitter, radio, TV, and the press—wherever you can get them. The reviewers and critics won't all love your stuff right away, unless you're very lucky. Just be happy they're talking about your project.

**CHALLENGE**

It's launch day for your new hip-hop and street dance company. What do you do to make it a success?

# Young Entrepreneur
## The Blair Witch Project

When it comes to launching a new movie on a small budget, you need to create an interest through word of mouth. Young filmmakers Daniel Myrick and Eduardo Sanchez had been working on their independent horror movie *The Blair Witch Project* for five years until they were ready to launch the film worldwide. The film is the story of three filmmakers investigating the legend of the Blair Witch in the Black Hills of Maryland, supposedly made from footage found after they had disappeared.

Before the launch, it was hinted that three people really had disappeared while making the movie and footage of their last days had been found. What's more, the message was spread on the Internet, which was becoming a great way to get news and stories out fast. Since then, this **viral** method has become widely used, but Daniel and Eduardo's film set the standard for successfully launching a small movie in the modern age. It cost about $750,000 to make and made $250,000,000—a massive profit!

**YOUR THOUGHTS**

Why was using the Internet a good way to launch this movie?

# How's It Going?

## Take Stock

Now that you've launched, you need to think about how you are doing. Look at all the aspects of your business and ask if you are doing the best you can. For example, you might wonder if you are in the right place. Is it the right theater for your play, a good club location for your comedy acts, or a helpful series of showcase venues for your group? It's never too late to make changes.

Similarly, if you've launched a product such as an online app, and you're selling through other outlets, are they the right ones for the type of people who might buy? Always double-check whether you're reaching your **target market**. Perhaps you would do better if you were to sell just through your own site. The main goal is to adjust any errors or mistakes as fast as you can.

**CHALLENGE**

How do you determine whether your online music service is doing as well as it could?

# Inspiring Entrepreneur
## Oprah Winfrey

For 25 years from 1986 to 2011, Oprah Winfrey hosted the most successful daytime TV talk show ever. It was produced by her company and aired around the world. Oprah's rise from poverty as a child to a position of huge power was the type of rags to riches story she loved to feature on the show.

Sent away by her mother to live with a man in Nashville she thought was her father, Oprah got a job on local radio while still in high school. She then became a news anchor on the local TV station, where her emotional delivery attracted attention. She was given the chance to take over as host of an unknown Chicago daytime TV talk show in early 1984. Within months, Oprah had turned it into the top-ranked show and was urged by a TV critic to launch the program nationally and to take over production. No one can deny she made a success of it. She was the first African American woman to become a billionaire.

**YOUR THOUGHTS**

How did Oprah know what she was doing was successful, and how did she build on this?

# Are You Keeping Everyone Happy?

## Team Spirits

The entertainment business is quite unusual in that there will often be business ideas, such as film companies or theater groups, which develop best when there is a form of profit sharing. Profit sharing is paying out the profits amongst the employees. This could happen as a **bonus** on top of salaries or in return for any financial investment that may have been made to the company.

Is profit sharing the right thing for your company? For you as the entrepreneur, you will think that you deserve a larger slice of the profit because you're running the greatest risk. But does this keep the team working well together? It's a tricky decision to make.

How else can you ensure that your team is happy and motivated? If profit sharing doesn't fit your business model, you may want to have field trips where everyone goes to a theme park or completes some fun activity together. Events like these are team builders and reward hard work. It's important that your team feels appreciated.

**CHALLENGE**

You've started a theater group where all the profits are shared. How do you make sure the money is paid out fairly when people make different contributions?

# Young Entrepreneurs

## Songkick

Songkick was founded in London in 2007 by three friends: Ian Hogarth, Michelle You, and Pete Smith. They noticed a gap in the market for finding out when their favorite bands and artists were coming to town. They set out to use information from ticket vendors, venue websites, and national and local media from around the world to build the Songkick website.

In three years, the team has increased from 7 to 23, and plenty of effort goes into making the employees feel valued. Everyone has the chance to share in the profits of the company on top of their wages. The whole team gets taken for days out and treated to special activities as a reward for their hard work. Add to that Yoga Wednesdays, a monthly movie night, and generous ticket allowances for concerts. The Songkick people really know how to keep their staff happy.

# Keep Moving Ahead

## Further Successes

Once you've achieved your goals, don't rest there. This is the time when real entrepreneurs continue to grow their business. And once you've experienced the thrill of your own bit of showbiz history, you'll probably want to do it all over again.

How can you best do this? There should be a natural link between the ideas you have, although it's not essential. If you're a DJ, should you be moving into record production? If you run a comedy club, might you try your hand at theater? Look at what you did successfully the first time around, and see how you can apply that to your new business. It's also sometimes good to go against the **trends**. For example, music seemed to be moving more and more into the background of TV, until a certain entrepreneur named Simon Cowell changed the whole game.

**CHALLENGE**

Your agency managing magicians has been very successful. Which other entertainers would you consider handling next?

# Inspiring Entrepreneur
## Simon Cowell

Simon Cowell from London, England, is now one of the most recognized faces on TV. He has been a judge on the British TV talent shows *Pop Idol, X Factor,* and *Britian's Got Talent,* along with the US counterparts *American Idol, X Factor,* and *America's Got Talent*. His production company, Syco, has produced all of these shows. It would be easy to think he's been in TV forever, but he hasn't.

In fact, Simon made his name as a producer and executive in the record industry working his way up from the mailroom at EMI (then a giant music publishing company). He had success with several companies before forming his own label, S-Records, and later, Syco Music. He had seen the problems that the music industry was facing—mainly the spread of digital music—and saw a gap in the market for joining music with TV. So he revived the TV talent show in a new way, and the rest is history.

**YOUR THOUGHTS**

Why do you think the TV talent shows have been so successful?

# Glossary

**advertising campaign** A series of images or stories that interest people in your product.

**backers** People who lend you money to help you start your business.

**bonus** Extra money you pay your staff for especially good and effective work.

**brand** A characteristic or trademark that identifies a product.

**budgeting** Figuring out the amount of money you expect to spend and receive.

**cash flow** The money coming in and going out.

**closed community** A group that no one else can enter.

**competitors** Everyone who is competing with you to sell to consumers.

**copyright** A legal way of stopping others from copying your product.

**costs** Everything you must spend to run your business.

**entrepreneur** Someone who takes a financial risk in order to make a profit.

**feedback** Comments on what you've said, made, or done.

**financial plan** Estimates of how much money you need and how much you'll make.

**indie** Independently produced, usually films or music not by a major studio or record label.

**investor** A person who put money into your business.

**launch** The moment you open your business or start selling your product.

**market research** Finding out if there's a market for your idea, or how your idea is doing.

**marketing plan** Describing your likely customers and how you'll sell to them.

**media** Newspaper, TV, radio, and the Internet.

**multimedia** A mixture of different media (such as print, film, TV, radio, and the Internet).

**potential market** A place or group where you are likely to find customers.

**primary research** Finding new information that is collected for the first time.

**product testing** What you do to make sure your product will be as good as possible.

**profit** The amount of money you receive for sales, minus the cost of making them.

**public relations (PR)** The work you do to give yourself a good reputation.

**publicity** The ways you get your business noticed in the media.

**risk** The chance of losing money invested in a business.

**rivals** Everyone who is competing with you to sell to consumers.

**secondary research** Finding information that already exists.

**target audience** The people you want to hear the messages about your products.

**target market** The people you want to interest in buying your products.

**trends** What is happening at the moment and is likely to happen in the future.

**user group** A special group set up to test a particular product.

**viral** Spreading information quickly (like a virus) by using the Internet.

# Further Information

## Web Sites of Featured Entrepreneurs

The Blair Witch Project
**www.blairwitch.com**
Cameron Mackintosh
**www.cameronmackintosh.com**
The DigiTour **http://thedigitour.com**
Footage Firm **www.footagefirm.com**
GaBoom **www.gaboomswap.com**
Glitch **www.glitch.com**
Lana Del Rey  **www.lanadelrey.com**

MakeBelieve Arts Music Arsenal
**www.musicarsenal.com/home**
Oprah Winfrey **www.oprah.com**
RKA Records **www.rkarecords.com**
SB.TV **http://sbtv.co.uk**
Sean Parker **www.foundersfund.com**
Selena Gomez **www.selenagomez.com**
Simon Cowell **www.sycocontact.com**
SongKick **www.songkick.com**

## Other Web Sites

**www.bbc.co.uk/dragonsden/**
Official web site of *Dragons' Den,* the British TV show, where you can see other budding entrepreneurs and the advice they receive.

**www.bbc.co.uk/youngapprentice**
Official web site of the *Young Apprentice* series, where youngsters try out their skills to succeed in business.

**www.youngentrepreneur.com/**
Online forum for information and advice on being a young entrepreneur.

## Books

*Entrepreneurship* by Rae Simons (Mason Crest Publishers, 2011)
*Built for Success: The Story of CNN* by Sara Gilbert (Creative Education, 2013)
*The Music Scene: The Music Industry* by Matt Anniss (Smart Apple Media, 2014)

**Note to parents and teachers:** Every effort has been made by the publishers to ensure that these web sites are suitable for children, and that they contain no inappropriate or offensive material. However, because of the nature of the Internet, it is impossible to guarantee that the contents of these sites will not be altered.

# Index